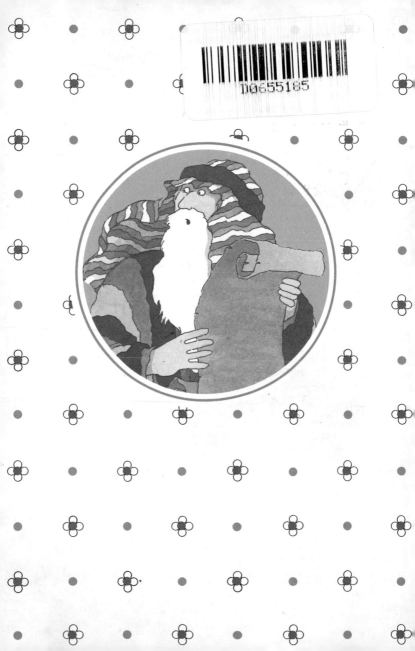

The story of Noah retold simply and
delightfully illustrated for young readers.

Note to parents and teachers
*It is traditional to present the story of Noah and the animals as one
full of comedy, even though its meaning is serious: God saves the
people who keep faith with him in an 'ark' of salvation. The story
of Noah also contains the first of God's great promises to man.
The full Biblical account of Noah and the flood can be found in
Genesis, chapter 6, verse 9 to chapter 9, verse 17.*

British Library Cataloguing in Publication Data
Hately, David
    Noah. — (Bible stories)
    1. Noah's ark — Juvenile literature
    I. Title   II. Breeze, Lynn   III. Bible.O.T.
    Genesis. *English. Selections. 1986*
    IV. Series
    222'.1109505   BS580.N6
    ISBN 0-7214-0992-X

First edition

Published by Ladybird Books Ltd Loughborough Leicestershire UK
Ladybird Books Inc Lewiston Maine 04240 USA

© LADYBIRD BOOKS LTD MCMLXXXVII

Printed in England

Noah

written *by* David Hately
illustrated *by* Lynn Breeze

Ladybird Books

God was angry. All the people who lived in the world he had made had forgotten him. They were selfish and cruel. They spent their days plotting wickedness.

God wanted to wash the whole world clean and so he decided to send a great flood.

Then he remembered that there was one man who *did* love him. The man's name was Noah.

God told Noah about the flood that he was going to send. 'You'll have to build an Ark,' God said.

Noah was puzzled. 'What is an Ark?' he asked. He began to get a bit worried when he heard that an Ark was like a big, wooden box that floated on water. There was nothing to make it go forwards or backwards; nothing to make it turn left or right; nothing to make it speed up or slow down. It just floated.

Noah thought that he would prefer to stay on dry land but God said that there wouldn't *be* any dry land. Noah scratched his chin. Perhaps the Ark wasn't a bad idea after all.

Then God told Noah how to build the Ark. It had to be three hundred cubits long.

'Three hundred cubits?' gasped Noah. 'A cubit is half as long as my arm. That makes the Ark *enormous*.'

Then God told Noah that it had to be fifty cubits wide and thirty cubits high. *And* there had to be a roof on it, because there would be a lot of rain.

Noah was gloomy. Building an Ark was going to be hard work.

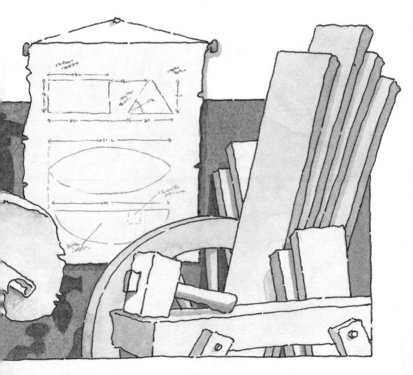

Then Noah remembered that he could share out the work. He had three sons! They could do the hard work, and he could do the planning.

When he learned that God wanted the Ark to be lined inside and out with pitch, Noah smiled happily.

'Pitch? That nasty, smelly black stuff? Looks like tar? No trouble. One of the boys can see to it.'

'And the whole Ark must be built from gopher wood,' God said.

'Ah! Yes! Gopher wood. Certainly. I'll sort it out right now.'

Noah's sons were all young married men. They were called Shem, Ham and Japheth.

'Now, lads,' said Noah, 'there's a little job I want you to do for me.'

Noah's sons groaned.

Luckily, Shem knew all about

gopher wood. He had built his house with it, he explained, because gopher wood didn't let in water during the wet season. 'You get it from up there,' he said, pointing to a hill.

'We'll need all of those trees,' said Noah. 'So you'd better get chopping!'

Noah scuttled into his house while his sons grumbled and groaned and went off to sharpen their axes.

In the weeks that followed God was pleased with Noah's work.

'Very good!' he said. 'But I think you'd better add a window. And the door must be high up in one side.'

God explained that if Noah left the door where it was, the water would get in when the Ark was afloat.

'You must put three decks inside the Ark,' God told Noah. 'Three floors.'

'But there are only eight of us!' cried Noah. 'My wife, my three sons, their wives… and me! What do we need three floors for?'

'Didn't I tell you?' said God. 'You'll be taking some passengers with you.'

Noah sent for his three sons.

'More wood!' he ordered. 'Lots more gopher wood. Go and chop!'

Wearily, the sons of Noah went off to sharpen their axes again.

At last the work was finished and
God came to inspect everything.
All the family gathered together.
Mrs Noah and the girls were wearing
their best clothes.

They all held their breath as God
looked round the Ark.

'Well done! It's a wonderful Ark!'
he said at last. 'Now!' he said.
'It's time to tell you about the
passengers.'

Silence fell.

'They're animals,' whispered God.

'Animals?' said Noah. '*Animals?* In my nice, new, gopher-wood Ark? **Animals**?'

'Only two of each kind,' said God.

Mrs Noah went pale.

'As well as animals,' God went on calmly, 'you'll be taking two each of all the birds, and two of everything that crawls.'

Shem's wife screamed. She didn't like things that crawled.

'To keep them all alive,' said God, 'you'll have to take all the different kinds of food they eat. Don't worry,' he added. 'It'll be all right. Trust me!'

Collecting all the animals and crawling things was bad enough, but catching the birds was a nightmare. They didn't want to be caught, and that was that.

Even when Noah *had* managed to get everything together, there were problems. The smaller things got trodden on. And the noise made by the elephants was tremendous.

The neighbours began to complain and Mrs Noah was very upset.

Next, all the food had to be
collected. Noah made a list.

'What do aardvarks eat?' he
shouted to Shem, who was hurrying
past with a couple of goats.

'What's an aardvark?' Shem yelled
back, not stopping to find out.

'I don't know,' wailed Noah, nearly
in tears. 'But it's top of my list!'

God had told them to start getting the animals on board the moment it started to rain.

The crawling things slithered up the sides of the Ark, two by two. The monkeys climbed up the ladder easily but the horses and dogs had a lot of trouble. Luckily, the birds flew in without making a fuss.

At last all the animals except the elephants were safe inside the Ark. Noah looked at the elephants. He looked at the high door. He looked at the wooden ladder. He looked at his sons.

'We've got a bit of a problem here, lads,' he said at last.

God solved the problem quite easily. The elephants were led away from the Ark and up a hill.

They waited there and watched as the water began to fill the little valley in which the Ark rested. The Ark began to move. First it wobbled, then it started bobbing up and down, and suddenly it was floating.

The Ark sank quite deeply into the water with the weight of all the animals inside it. When it reached the hillside the elephants were able to step straight in.

'Now don't be afraid,' God said as he shut the doors up behind them all. 'I won't forget about you. Trust me!'

As the Ark floated away, the animals set up such a barking and bellowing and howling and miaowing and hissing and cackling and trumpeting.

Higher and higher rose the flood waters. And, remembering what a loving friend God had been to himself and his family, Noah wept.

For a while the Ark passed islands of rock. These were the mountain tops of the earth. But soon there was nothing at all to be seen from the window except water. Even the mountains had been covered over.

At last it stopped raining. After forty days afloat Noah decided to find out if the water was going down.

He whistled for a raven. Noah whispered in the bird's ear, stroked its black feathers, and let it fly away.

For a day or two Noah and his family could see it. But it didn't come back to them.

'It must be getting hungry,' sobbed Japheth's wife, who had grown fond of all the birds. 'Why doesn't it come back?'

But Noah and his sons knew that ravens were able to feed on the carcasses of dead animals floating on the water. They knew that the bird would never return to them.

A few days later, Noah sent out a
dove. But it soon returned to the Ark.
They knew that it had found nowhere
to perch. The land was still covered in
water.

A week later, Noah tried again.
This time the dove stayed away for
the whole day. But in the evening
there was a sudden flurry of wings
and there it was, flying towards the
Ark.

'Look!' cried Noah.

In its beak, the dove was carrying a leaf. They could see that it had been freshly torn from an olive bush. The bird had found dry land!

Another week passed, and again Noah sent the dove out. This time it didn't return. Noah and his sons were happy, knowing that they would soon be able to leave the Ark.

Next morning they threw open the window of the Ark and looked out. There was still plenty of water but now there was dry land too!

God had not forgotten them. He came to Noah and said, 'Now you can all leave the Ark. As for the animals, the birds, and the crawling things... let them come out as well!'

And what a marvellous sight it was as the animals trooped out, stopping now and then to sniff the scents of the new world, breathing good fresh air after weeks inside the stuffy Ark.

As soon as Noah had got everybody onto dry land, he began to build an altar with some rocks and stones.

The animals were all there as Noah and his family offered prayers of thanks to God who had watched over them and kept them safe inside the Ark. Afterwards, most of the animals began drifting away.

At last, Noah and his family were alone. Well, not quite alone. They never did manage to get the cats and dogs to leave them so they became the family pets.

God was pleased that Noah had remembered to thank him for saving them. And then he made a wonderful promise.

'I will never again destroy the things I have made,' he said. 'No matter how selfish, how cruel, how wicked people may become, I will never send another flood to wipe them out. Look at the sky!' God said. 'There is the sign that I will keep my promise!'

Noah and his family gasped as they saw the shimmering colours of the very first rainbow.

'Whenever it rains,' God said, 'and the rainbow appears in the clouds, you will remember my promise and know that the rain will soon stop.

'Now go and fill the world with your children,' he said to them all, 'and teach them to be the people of God!'

Noah and his family sat quietly
after God left them. They were
looking at the rainbow and thinking
about God's promise.

The girls were trying to get used to
the idea of having God as a friend.
They had known nothing about him
until they married the Noah boys, and
were still shy with him.

But soon the cats were miaowing,
and the dogs were barking and
wagging their tails. Nearby there were
ducks quacking, and hens clucking.

'Must be supper time!' said Noah,
standing up and stretching. 'Come on,
all of you! It's time to begin life.'